BACK STREETS

Marvin,
Great to meet a brother
who portrays dignity

Chali Jones
11-9-20

Palmetto Publishing Group
Charleston, SC

Back Streets: They Didn't See us Cry
Copyright © 2018 by James "Chali" Jones
All rights reserved

First Edition

Printed in the United States

ISBN-13: 978-1-64111-197-3
ISBN-10: 1-64111-197-6

BACK

STREETS

THEY DIDN'T SEE US CRY

A MEMOIR

JAMES "CHALI" JONES

(A/K/A FATIH AL-AMIN)

CHAPTER 1

AS MY SONS, Tim and Dameon, and I started down the steps that led to what was, to me, all the stories of hell contained in two single-row tenement flats, appropriately named Stall Pool Court. I say appropriately because, upon my arrival here at the age of six, my mental development was stalled in a pool of hate, fear and jealous rage eating at the people who lived here. What had been my initiation into a neighborhood torn by the after effects of racism, disillusionment and poverty, was now only broken soil. As I remembered my first days here, I looked at my son Dameon, who was the age I was at the time, and a warm feeling of thankfulness swept over me, for the rot of human activity which had ensnarled me would not have to be his or his brother's lot.

"This is where I used to live when I first came to Lexington fellas. I used to sit right here by this telephone pole at night," I told them, as I pointed to the pole which stood in the middle of the empty lot. I had taken refuge beside this pole the first night my family moved from Atlanta, Georgia. All I remember about that night was that I couldn't understand why I was ridiculed and laughed at by the bully known as "Bubbles" who lived next door. He kept throwing rocks at me and snickering. What had I done? I'd only known happiness in the short span of my life in Atlanta. To me, Atlanta had been family, friends, a big back yard and driveway. Before my father had left home so abruptly, I had known only things that a young boy at the vulnerable age of five could learn. When my mother said she was looking for a job, my mind automatically told me that she meant "jar." Why did grown-ups go out looking for a jar?! I'd always been mischievous but only to the point of throwing dirt in my sister Jean's hair and running up a small tree until I was told to come down for my "whoopin'." This command usually came from my older sister Ruth, who always babysat us when Momma wasn't home.

One day, though, I noticed that Momma was selling the furniture and talking about going to some place called Kentucky. Daddy had gone to Kentucky where he had a sister who was doing fine. We'd been there once before and I had fun playing on what I thought was the busiest street I'd ever see – Georgetown Street. I was too young to really miss Atlanta so I didn't mind the long bus ride, even though I'd regurgitated on some poor lady's feet on the way. I was really sick.

I guess I'd miss going to Lawrenceville and seeing my grandmother. I'd miss going to the spring and getting cool fresh water. I'd miss the pine forests and my cousins always calling me Chali James. I'd miss my beautiful red dirt. I'd miss the fresh smell of logs on the fire. I'd miss those large country breakfasts and melt-in-your mouth biscuits grandma used to make (just the thought made my mouth water even now). Uummm.

"Daddy, what happened to your house?" Dameon asked, bringing me back to the present. "Man, I didn't live in a house; those were apartments." Tim, being older, simply looked around hoping to find something to get in to.

This had been my first return here for at least seventeen years. Though I had lived in the same town I had never had the urge to go back. But I don't know why. I would live in some worse places. The bulldozers had done their work to the land but nothing could take it from my mind.

Looking around, I found that the surroundings were the same. The houses, with their backs facing us, were still well fenced from this back-alley section. I'd never noticed how we'd been surrounded on all sides by other people's backyards. On one side was Chestnut, then Breckinridge which intersected with

Shropshire. Sixth Street was at the back of the building I used to live in. Between that building and Sixth was Scott's Roll Arena where I spent many hours learning to be one of the hippest skaters around. The big castle-like house still stood beside the skating rink. It was so big! I never knew who owned it but it was huge. I think it was always rented in sections, unless there used to be a rich white family that owned it. I know there weren't any black families that rich around there at that time. And, if there were, I didn't know any. I'd never thought of myself as poor, though me and the other kids in the neighborhood had stolen bottles from neighbor's porches or candy from the store. In fact, there was never anything that we couldn't steal to make some money. We even fought to determine who would win the treasures found on the porches of our neighbors. The danger of getting caught made it exiting. The chase was the best part. Sometimes while running away, I'd laugh until my stomach hurt at how easily I out-distanced anyone on my trail. What fun! I never considered that we did it because we were hungry. To me, excitement was the way of life on Stall Pool Court.

One early Thursday evening Bubbles, Otha Jean, Jo Jo, Milton, Junebug, Tubby and I were standing under the light pole in the middle of the unit where I lived when we heard the cry of a woman and jumped at the prospect of a good fight. This wasn't even the weekend so we were really excited as we headed towards the noise coming from the Trombone family's window. The Trombones were an almost-white family who had quietly moved into the neighborhood from the hills of Kentucky (or so I thought). Most of the almost-white folks were said to come from the "hills" where blacks and whites lived together in harmony, or so we thought.

"Don't cut him! No, no -- please no!" Mrs. Trombone was screaming at someone. The sound of dishes breaking made us eagerly strain to hear and see the action, though fights were commonplace around the neighborhood. The sound of breaking glass, along with Mrs. Trombone's screams, brought more people to the scene.

"Please don't cut him," she screamed! Mrs. Trombone and the noise stopped as suddenly as it had started. Someone shouted, giving the signal that the action was coming that way. Mr. Trombone had run out the back door and made it to the parking lot at the end of the Court. He fell and was holding his stomach as his shirt turned crimson with blood. He'd been badly cut and was unable to talk. Another tenant from the end apartment attempted to comfort him as he groaned and heaved in pain on the asphalt lot. Someone called the rescue squad to the scene but it hadn't arrived and you could hear the gossip among the people in the neighborhood.

Miss Mary Lou, who always drank a lot and gossiped as though she were an authority on everything, was talking to Otha's mother, Miss Bessie Lee. "She been goin' out on him all along," she attempted to whisper, though several people heard the remark anyway.

Someone had seen Rev. Roach slip out the back door and go in the other direction as Mr. Trombone had come out in shock. Rev. Roach was a part-time preacher who had who-knows how many kids and Mrs. Trombone, being new in the neighborhood, must have been fooled by his smooth manner. He was a large, dark man with the then-popular processed hair, which made me think of him as a ladies' man. His strong deep voice gave him the image of strength. He was a bricklayer during the week.

Mrs. Trombone, like so many of the women, had what the fellas called a "hot tail" for the smooth-talking men of the neighborhood. She was one of many "country-type" women that moved in the neighborhood who weren't hip to the well-practiced lines of the weekend dandies who worked all week and dressed up on the weekends to show off their sharpest "fits," which were usually purchased with the hard-earned money of their wives or girlfriends.

By the time the ambulance finally arrived, a large crowd had gathered and the onlookers buzzed with the excitement of something happening. Mr. Trombone was barely conscious at this point and the only sign of life in his bloodied body was an occasional groan. Mrs. Trombone, along with her four children, Joyce, the oldest and prettiest with long brown hair and grey eyes (during that period in my life I was more "white-feature" programmed), Sandra, no less attractive but with more black features, Daryle and Philpot, the baby, were all crying hysterically. Mrs. Trombone was doing a poor job of covering her shame. Everyone was aware of what was going on. Mr. Trombone had multiple stab wounds and later recovered but his family never got back together. The children were later put into an orphanage.

It was as if a great thing had happened because, after the ambulance whisked Mr. Trombone away, everyone was espousing his or her point of view, with the older or more experienced forcing their view of what had occurred on the younger or less opinionated people in the crowd. Everyone in the neighborhood knew each other because the two rows of brick tenements were only about a half block long. The so-called religious of the neighborhood could be heard testifying, "The Laud gon' be here soon chile! God knows we can't live in sin and violence!" The non-churchgoers could be heard stating their point of view – from "I wish I caught a nigga with my wife I'd a killed his ass," to "I'd a killed *her* if it was me!" The kids in the neighborhood were still excited by what had just occurred. We had something to talk about that night. Soon, the crowd slowly dispersed and Miss Fanny, a big motherly woman, took it upon herself to look in on the Trombone kids for the night. Mrs. Trombone had gone with the ambulance.

We went back to our light pole to discuss the night's events. Bubbles, being the oldest and more so the leader since he was with us younger boys, bragging "Man, ain't nobody go'n come in my house and do that to me. I'd put that bitch out man, hell yeah!" "Me too, man. Shit. Yeah jack," were the echoes as we imitated and tried to be and sound cool like Bubbles.

I finally eased away and went in for the night as I was not allowed to stay out late yet. The others either stayed and talked or drifted off into some mischief for the night. The fellas who were able to stay out ranged in age from around nine years and up. Many of the parents on Stall Pool

Court didn't care how long their kids were out or what they did. Many of the older boys and girls had been on their own and came and went as they pleased since they were about thirteen. Many of the kids either had just a mother and a lot of siblings or a mother and father who drank a lot and really didn't care what they did.

Our family was usually nice, normal to me. My father was never a staggering drunk as were so many of the fathers in the neighborhood. However, on many occasions, I had witnessed him taking a drink from a wine bottle he used to keep in the refrigerator. I was to learn later that the wine he drank was one of the cheapest, gut-rotting kind. I never heard my father or mother curse at each other or around us kids. I learned to curse in the street. My father, James Jones, Sr., was a baker but he never owned his own bakery. He never seemed to prosper, but at my age, all that I saw was a tall, strong and loving father.

Though it was well hidden, he and my mother must have had more fights than I had seen. They had three that I can recall, none of which was very serious. No one was hurt physically. My six year-old mind wasn't aware of any more than comic books, which I looked at from front to back, daily adventure, marbles and fighting. I was even aware of girls. I tried to get any lil' girl I could to play house with me. I never thought that anything was wrong in my family or the way we lived.

I remember one of the worst beatings I ever received. I had gone to Griffith's Market on Sixth Street and stolen a cake. I was so excited at my growing adventure that I hurried home to tell my mother. She calmly listened as I told her. Mike, a friend who'd been with me, disappeared out the back door. I thought that her arm would never stop.

Although things were rough, one learns to adapt and life becomes normal. I soon became one of the best thieves and could curse with any-one. I was good at anything that I concentrated on. I received attention on many fronts. I learned early to respect my elders. I tried to keep my ac-tivities a secret to some people. To those who saw me as a thief, I was a thief. To the teacher, I was an angel. I was good in school from the beginning. After my mother taught me otherwise, I'd thought that everything was all right – even stealing. I learned that the adults praised you if you were of honorable character. I learned at the age of six about the larceny of life.

CHAPTER 2

BEFORE I ENTERED the second grade, my family moved again. Fate would have it that the bitter would be followed by the sweet. We moved to Georgetown Street. My new friends, Snag, Ken T., Bub, Beadie Mo and the whole gang, seemed different. It was on the west side of town. Our house was no better but I had a little yard. It was a straight-back wooden house. They are commonly known as shot-gun houses. I thought we were doing better. The house that my Aunt Ruth had lived in was only three houses over. Snag's family lived next door. His father, David Combs, Sr., was a painter and appeared to be affluent. He owned our house. Their house was big with a wide concrete porch. Snag had three sisters, Majorette (the oldest), Nancy (next to Majorette and the prettiest), and Fay (the baby). Ken T., whose real name was Kenneth T. Smith, and Bub lived next door to Snag. Their father, Mr. Smith, worked out of town and came home on the weekends. Mrs. Smith was very motherly, plump and humorous. They also had an older sister named Viv. Since I was only seven and Ken T. and Bub were about thirteen, I didn't see much of Viv. Their family was very warm and close. I spent as much time at their house as I could. As young as we were, some of the older boys took us kids under their wing and taught us how to play ball, swim in a creek, shoot a bow and arrow and many other things a youngster needs to know growing up. Ken T. was my own personal hero. Even though I had an older brother, he wasn't into sports or anything. He was into girls and had a sharp car. I always wanted to be like my brother and Ken T. when I grew up.

The biggest influence in my life had to be Ken T. of all the older guys in the group. Ken T. had to be the most level-headed. He always seemed to have time to show me how to do something. I was even bat-boy for his and Bub's little league baseball team. Ken T. made me feel as though I was his little brother.

My closest friends in West End didn't steal like my former running mates. They were from different family backgrounds and didn't put much emphasis on stealing and fighting. I still stole an occasional ice cream sandwich or cake. We loved to play ball and hike. I got my first real bike at the age of eight. It was a three-speed racer. I was the envy of the group that Christmas.

I remember huddling around the fireplace in the winter with the family. We even had mice. They seemed to come and go at will. I saw my brother Barry trap five in a row in one evening. Life to me was still playing ball, hiking, marbles and girls. I've always wanted to fool with the girls.

My second-grade teacher, Miss Lewis, was the most beautiful lady I'd ever seen. Since I was very intelligent and tough, I was her pet. We had a bully in class named Freddie Hayes. Miss Lewis couldn't even handle him. With my Stall Pool Court experience, I was the one for the job so sometimes Miss Lewis would let me fight with Freddie so the class could see that he wasn't as tough as he tried to appear. I could beat anybody in the class.

One day, I tried not to appear to be watching but I knew something was wrong when Mrs. Didley, the school principal, came into class and whispered something in Miss Lewis's ear and they both looked at me. I hadn't done anything wrong so what was making them look so urgent? I started feeling scared when looked out the window and saw the fire trucks. Booker T. Washington Elementary was only half a block from my house and, from the look on their faces, I knew they were at my house. At lunch time, I sneaked away from school and ran home, where my worst fears were confirmed. Our back porch and kitchen had been badly burned. I learned later that my brother Barry had placed a box of smoldering ashes from the fireplace on the porch. For the next few weeks, we had to stay in different homes until we could find another place.

We moved to Bright Avenue. It was just on the other side of the school yard but was more of an alley than a street. I remember it had only three rooms and no bathroom. We'd bathe in a big steel tub or wash from the wash basin. The toilet was in the back yard. Even though Bright Avenue wasn't much better than Stall Pool Court, the people weren't as bad. There wasn't any fighting among the adults. To me, life wasn't bad but with nine people sharing three rooms, it had to be rough. We lived there until the early part of my third-grade year before we moved back to the east side of town.

CHAPTER 3

OUR NEW NEIGHBORHOOD was
a dead-end street called Holbrook Court. It was
more of an alley, although there was a sidewalk
the length of the six-house court. These houses were much better in comparison to Bright
Avenue and I had that little-boy hope to have a
real home. As it turned out, our house was just as
crowded with every room of the four-room house
being used as sleeping rooms as well. My father,
my younger brother Cledi and I shared the same

bed in the back of the house. My mother and younger sister Jean slept in the middle room, along with my baby sister Vernita. My older sister Ruth slept in the living room with my niece Vern, and my older brother Barry slept on the couch. Barry, being older, must have taken as much as he could because after only a short while there he left and went back to Atlanta. Being so young, I really didn't miss him but I'd still brag to my companions that I had one of the sharpest brothers anywhere. Barry had been a very clean-cut and hardworking young man. He worked for an uncle on his construction crew – the only relatives we had in Lexington were an aunt and uncle, who never came to visit. Uncle Rev and Aunt Ruth had bought a house in the newly-developed black suburb known as St. Martin's Village. I thought they were rich. Barry also had a lot of pretty girlfriends and I wanted to be just like him.

Living on Holbrook Court was a continuation of street knowledge. Whereas I'd been subjected to a broader range of people on Georgetown Street and happened to be closely associated with people considered to be well-to-do now I was back in the midst of street influences. Though I still played a lot of sports and got along very well in school, I was learning how to smoke. I was around free sex. Everyone – I thought – knew about "doing it." I'd never seen my parents "do it" but I still knew what a little girl had. My new friends on the street and around the neighborhood were mostly poor like me so there was always the comfort of having like circumstances at home.

My next-door neighbors, the Andersons, were my new influence. Janice, the oldest, was very good looking and had a nice body. I'd secretly watch some of her friends' sex parties. Her brother Johnny was next in age and was always a nice guy. Gary, who became my running partner, followed by Blanche, who was my sweetheart, Norris and little Donna. They didn't live with their father, and their mother, Miss Lula Mae, worked a lot. She was a large woman and was never overly nice. The Andersons did just about whatever they pleased so my sister Jean and I would be over to their house as much as possible. Though there were numerous kids in the neighborhood, I spent the largest portion of my time with Johnny or Gary. Norris wasn't able to hang with us that much yet.

I spent the rest of my elementary school years on Holbrook Court. My life was still that of a poor child but to me it couldn't have been better. The days were filled with sports, stealing, hiking, bike riding and girls; all the things that a boy was supposed to have, I thought I had. I got another bike for Christmas; I had a charge account for all the doughnuts I wanted at the bakery, which was just across the street from where we lived. I'd been helping my father off and on at the bakery since we'd been in Lexington. By the time I was in the sixth grade, I could jump a train and ride for a block or two and jump off, jump from the top of a train into the sand at a cement plant where we loved to play, smoke, steal, curse and shoot dice. Along with my outside activities, I was an honor student and was a member of group skits, a modern dance show and had been on television. My father bought a 1952 Ford. I saw my parents fight only once during our habitation on Holbrook Court.

My mother was always religious and my family belonged to church – that is, all except me. I never got up enough nerve to march down the aisle in church and confess my sins before so many people. My father would sometimes drop me off at church and I'd sneak to the park as soon as I could. My family belonged to Liberty Baptist Church on Chestnut St. pastored by Rev. Lee. Rev Lee was an old school fire and brimstone preacher. He stayed sharp and drove a new cadillac. He was a light skin man and had a gold tooth. On Sunday mornings his preaching would have the women shouting and falling out all over the place. This used to really scare me. Momma used to shout to. Shouting in the black church is when someone caught the holy spirit and seemed to just lose control of themselves. Out of nowhere they would just start jumping and crying, maybe running and convulsing. This is common in the black Baptist church.

I started studying music in the fourth grade and was an outstanding percussion student. Mr. Quillings was my music teacher. He was a brilliant musician. My parents never took up much time with me on school matters but things in school were a breeze to me.

Though my parents were from the deep south – my mother was from Georgia and my father was from Alabama – I never heard much about white people or paid much attention to them. My mother always taught us that education was the key to success. "Get a trade and work for yourself if it is possible," she'd say. To hear her tell it, white folks were dirty. She meant their ways. It may seem strange to many but I was unconscious of race until I was about twelve years old. I always thought of myself as a Negro – at least that's what I heard other folks say. Referring to oneself as "black" was ridiculed around 1960. Since I was a Negro of color, I simply took it that the while folks, who didn't have any color, were "niggers." No one told me any different. I learned a different story later.

One fall evening when I was in the fifth grade, Norris, Moochie, some of the fellas and myself were wrestling in the Charles Young Park when I felt a piece of glass go into my knee. I wasn't aware of how bad it was and it didn't feel as though it was more than a minor cut. Blood was really spurting and it made me feel tough to bleed like that. I had never been hurt bad and it looked rugged to me. I walked home from the park with Norris and Moochie tagging behind. It was only about three blocks up Third Street and we had to pass Cottrell's Foodliner and Bakery to get there. So, thinking about the tasty delights and displaying my battle wound, I marched into the store with my fellow combatants noisily in tow. When we got to where my father worked making doughnuts in the back, he took a look at my knee and dismissed it at a glance. In no real pain, I joined my partners in looking for my choice of treats. Daddy, knowing something was amiss, got us a bag of a variety of sweet meats and we went routinely about the business of devouring our share. When I got home, Momma checked me out and feigning a scowl, rolled her eyes and in her southern manner stated, "Boy, I always tell you not to be down there fightin'! I got enough trouble as it is!" Retorting in my spoiled way and enjoying the attention, I blurted, "Aw momma, I'm all right."

I went to bed as usual with no pain at all. When momma woke me for school the next morning, the stiffness and pain in my knee had me howling in tearful anguish as soon as I attempted to move. The pain in my knee was so great that I couldn't move or bend it at all. My father was at home and he and momma were discussing whether to take me to the hospital or not. Daddy, after working all night, was undoubtedly tired so the final admonition was that I was to remain home to see if it got better. He and momma exchanged a few heated words but I never went to the hospital, though it took my knee a long time to heal. There was pain and stiffness for months. Since being in Lexington, I'd learned to keep quiet about things happening to me because my parents seemed to have enough problems as it was.

Later, the winter of that same year, I was bitten by a rat as I slept but, because it was only a finger scratch, I never told momma or daddy about it. Many incidents that happened to me, such as fights and trouble that I got into while in the streets, went unreported at home.

The first trouble I had that could be considered serious by my folks was the summer of my sixth-grade school year. I was engrossed in watching some older guys shoot dice at the park. "Shoot a dollar!" "You faded!" Bet one you lose!" "Hell man, you can't do that shit!" The chatter was fast and furious as I tried as best I could to catch on. Before anyone became aware of it, we were spied by Mr. John Will Brown, the park director. "Stop! Don't nobody run; I know you!" Realizing that he did know me, I was too scared to move. Two guys named Cheese and Price and I were the only ones left after the remaining fellows scattered. Cheese was very big and dark and could have easily gotten away. Price probably could have too but he didn't move. John Will, as we called him, seemed furious as he said, "I'm getting sick and damned tired of you hoodlums gambling in the park. This time, I'm going to do something about it!" As he was verbally chastising us, he led us to the city owned station wagon and loaded us in. The trip to the police station was quick and before I knew it, I was staring as innocently as possible at the officer as he booked us in. It was really minor and they let momma come take me home. What adventure! Here was my first brush with the law. Daddy really didn't say much and life continued as usual.

CHAPTER 4

BY THE TIME I was out of elementary school, I was considered a very bright student and, upon entering junior high, was expected to be just as studious and good in school. I was expected to excel at anything I tried. We moved to Maple Avenue from Holbrook Court and the large two-story frame house was the best looking we had lived in yet. It was occupied by two families. Mr. Joe and his wife Clarice didn't have children. They lived upstairs. It was much nicer than anything we'd lived in and there were mostly whites living in the large houses on this street. I guess Daddy wasn't a good businessman because after only a little while we had to move again. We moved right next door. It was a large two-story brick house. A white family lived upstairs.

Life was much the same but playing with the white kids was a lot different. We got along well as youngsters but I thought them to be awfully square. Their parents, though not outright hostile, kept to their own. I never noticed any friendly exchanges between them and my parents.

I remember playing with a football one night with Phil, the boy upstairs, his sister Evelyn, and their cousin Donna, in the front yard. The object was to take the ball away from whoever had it. As we screamed and tumbled around the yard, I began to notice the girls eyeing me. Each time I'd try and take the ball, they'd strategically place it between the crotch of their legs. The only way I could get the ball away was to rub right there in that spot or touch it in some way.

I was so into the game that I didn't notice Keith Walker, a boy I'd known for some time, come into the yard until he asked, "Can I play?" The word "no" almost escaped my mouth. I was so close to getting my first white girl that I didn't want anything to mess it up. Donna, who didn't look quite as good as Evelyn, said, "Yeah." Since no one else objected, Keith jumped right into the game. The game lasted only a little longer and Keith, who wasn't hip, had spoiled all my plans. My chance for some white stuff went down the drain at the insistence of Keith playing a rough and tumble game instead of feeling his way along as I was.

The inevitable of American society happened on Maple Street. A little white girl from down the street and I were arguing when it happened. "You a nigger 'cause my daddy says so," she stated in an authoritative manner. Since I'd never been called a nigger, or even knew what one was, I retorted, "I'm a Negro. You're a nigger 'cause you ain't got no color!" "No, I'm not. You are," she screamed! "You're a nigger," I said as I stood calling the shocked little girl a white nigger. That is as near as I've come in my life to a face-to-face confrontation with a white person calling me names or belittling me.

One day, when the whole family was in the house, Daddy and Momma began to argue. Jean and the younger ones were all scared. Ruth and I were scared but we still kept a close eye on things. I was on the bed between Momma and Daddy when suddenly Daddy attempted to hit Momma. I don't recall much after that but his arm never hit its mark. Ruth and I sprang into action at the same time and Daddy was lying on his back where we'd knocked him down. My Daddy was a big man, standing over six feet. The children were all crying and Momma looked kind of silly, or shocked maybe. Ruth and I were screaming at him, "You better not hit her again or I'll knock your head off." I was surprised at my courage. Daddy's look was blank. I guess he finally got over the shock because he told me to shut up, which I promptly did. That was the last time I saw my parents have an argument.

Not long afterward, that same summer of my hiatus between sixth and seventh grades, Jean told me that Momma was in the car with another man. I was immediately irate. I couldn't believe it. I followed Jean up the street to the corner and to my surprise and disbelief found her accusation to be true! They were only talking but still I looked at Momma as if she were a traitor. I guess Daddy had kept his actions hidden better. I never saw him with anyone else. Later, after the bald-headed man in the big black car had visited with Momma a couple times, I flattened his tires when he'd come to the house while Daddy was at work. Maybe Daddy knew about it. I never would have told him, even though I loved him very much.

Later that summer, things came to a head between my parents because we moved and left Daddy standing on the back porch of that big house one warm, dusky evening. Bitterness would soon start to set in on me and a hardening of my insides began to intensify beyond what had taken place on Stall Pool Court. We were never to be a complete family again. I was too young to understand the feelings of the others. All I knew was that my life was being torn apart.

CHAPTER 5

WE MOVED TO Rand Avenue in the northern part of town. There were whites in this neighborhood as well. We moved to a wooden white duplex and had only three small rooms on either side. This was to be the beginning of my career in crime. It was not serious yet but, because of the absence of my father, I had only the influence of the streets. Momma couldn't control me. I was entering seventh grade and at a very insecure stage in my life. Now more than ever the influence of a father was needed. My bitterness was shielded by a veneer of cool.

Prior to this time, I had been an excellent student but the breakup of my family had taken all thoughts of study from my mind. I even stopped playing the drums. I got through my seventh-grade year without failing. Now, it was time to go to high school. At that time, blacks in the seventh grade went to Dunbar Annex, which was two blocks from Dunbar High School. We couldn't wait to go to school at Dunbar High School, which touted the best basketball and football teams in the state (black or white), or so we thought. Dunbar Annex was a conglomeration of all the black seventh graders in town that would not be attending the white schools. We thought no one but "squares" attended the white schools or, even worse, the "bourgeois niggas."

I had started to go to social dances and, drinking wine; I was fully aware of the opposite sex and becoming more of a terror by the day. My family moved once again from three crowded rooms on Rand Avenue to two rooms, kitchen and bathroom on Georgetown Street in an apartment building called Jones' Apartments. From our many moves, I was already known in most of the black neighborhoods of Lexington.

CHAPTER 6

THOUGH MY FAMILY was poor, it still didn't register or I tried to fantasize it away. I'd never been exposed to any better. My bitter fight had only begun. My interest in my family was only the acknowledgement of having one. I would take up for them. Cledi was too young to hang with me. We hadn't had a family picnic or a family get together since early in my life. When Daddy was with us, he'd take us out for Sunday drives or visiting friends but Momma had so much responsibility after he left that any type of real family recreation was out of the question. My sister Ruth, being of the social age and saddled with two children, probably was really in a slump. I never noticed these things.

My friends, as before, didn't steal as we had on the east side of town. On the east side, we were hustlers. I stole candy and goodies of that sort every chance I could. I hadn't been caught yet. I'd been in skirmishes with the fellows many times which at that time I thought was fun. The chase itself was often times more exciting than the stealing. Now, I realize that there was so little to go around after we left Daddy. I didn't even realize that the people around us looked down on us because we were poor. My friends were just as poor. My mother taught us to be proud anyway.

It seems odd now when I reminisce; my father was a baker and my mother a beautician. Both trades can be very profitable. Both my parents could have made as much money as any professional in town but still we never prospered in Lexington as we did in Atlanta.

Maybe we hadn't prospered in Atlanta but I didn't know.

My father left town during the time we lived in Jones Apartments. Now, it appeared as if Lexington had completed the breakup of our family structure. We'd come from a large city to a small town only to regress to such a state. Because we were so young, except for Ruth, we weren't conscious of just how lowly our status had become, which was good since we always had the sense that we were as good as anyone else.

Once when I was home by myself, Mr. Graves, the big red-faced white landlord, came to collect the rent. Momma must have been behind on rent because I remember him telling me in a heated and vulgar way to tell my mother that if we didn't have the money when he came back that he was going to "kick the whole damn kit and caboodle out in the middle of Georgetown Street." I was seething while fighting back burning tears. I wanted to smash him to his knees with all my small thirteen-year old frame.

Before I finished my seventh- grade year, we moved back to East End to Hawkins Avenue.

The reputation of Hawkins Avenue was the same as Stall Pool Court and, like Stall Pool Court, was a back alley. Many, if not all, of the residents who lived there originated from Stall Pool Court. Hawkins Avenue consisted of one block of "shotgun houses." "Shotgun houses" were built straight back and narrow. Most of them are single story but our house was two-story. Our move to Hawkins Avenue brought my bitterness to the fore. The rage in me built up to the boiling point. There was no return. At this point in my life, the revolt began. At the beginning of my eighth-grade year, I became a real rebel. In no way did I envision the anguish and hurt that was to come.

No, I felt, as I looked at my two small sons. No, you won't have to see it as I did. "Daddy can we go," Tim asked? "Yeah man, let's go," I said turning to leave the empty lot while blinking back the tears.

CHAPTER 7

WE ALL WANT to be acknowledged. To matter, it seems, is universal. In some way the individual the world over has this desire. In my community we place value on material possessions of little consequence, such as big rims on our cars, clothes we can't afford, cheap ostentatious jewelry. All simply, to be seen. All to say, "I matter."

I'm dealing here with the black community. I'm dealing with what I know from my experience. Primarily I was to share the black male experience from a broken perspective. This perspective is one that has been shared by so many of us over the years. To try and make sense of the attack on our psyche that we encounter as soon as we are able to comprehend and make sense of this life. This awareness usually begins about the time of puberty. I was called a nigger to my face for the first time at the age of twelve. The young white girl that did it was just saying what she had heard at home; I'm sure. I didn't actually didn't know what a nigger was; and I'm from Georgia. The occurrence was in Kentucky. Much later in life I was called a nigger by a drunk, white boy who I couldn't get at. I would have busted his punk ass head.

I want to share what the vast majority of my brothers of color can't articulate. Our people don't put the premium on literacy that is called for in this society. We forget that there was a time when the law in many areas of this country forbade a black person from learning to read and write. The social reasoning behind such a law was that it's hard to enslave literate people. It's almost impossible to control the mind of someone capable of critical thought and analysis. I will; from my perspective; relate the experience, the hurt, the drug dependence, the irresponsibility, the depression and the anger of the black male growing up in America from the 1950's and to try and shed light on a world not seen by society as a whole. I will also relate the strength, the guile, the stamina and the wisdom that has brought us through the American experience as seen by a poor black man. A man to be known as an American of African descent.

Reading has been my escape. Reading has been my elevation, my transformation, my ascendency in being. Reading has allowed me to relate to the likes of Socrates, King Solomon of biblical times, Fredrick Douglas, Malcolm X, Abe Lincoln, Henry David Thoreau and on and on and on. All the great thinkers are within reach. Being able to read and comprehend has been my lifeline to transformation. To study the words of Jesus and the universality of his wisdom has been as tonic to my spirit. Having read the life stories of people whose lives were so much bleaker than my own gave me perspective. Having read the life story of Nelson Mandela showed me that holding on to the vengeance, anger and hate stifled inner growth. Booker T. Washington showed me a practicality that can be used today in my community. When I was in the 4th grade I worked in the library at Constitution Elementary School. Mrs. Greene was the librarian and she really took a liking to me. She prompted me to read a book called The Bronze Bow by Elizabeth George Speare. From then on I have always been for the underdog. I've always wanted to fight for the cause of the downtrodden. There have also been gangsta books about the hood. I'm into that genre, but there is so much more to my intellect than to dwell at that level. I read those types of books more for entertainment than enlightenment. Philosophy and critical thinking inspires my study at this point in my life.

All these great men and so many more have nurtured my mind and spirit over the years.

From making mistake, after mistake, after mistake, I can say that there is some wisdom in this head of mine. The truth is that there have been great men of color throughout the history of the world. One would say, though, the conqueror tells history from his point of view. The history I have learned through the years has been through the lens of the white Euro-American focus. As an American of African descent I have had to do the necessary research and study to find my place in the society I was born into. I have been bombarded with such nonsense as to say we as a people are somehow inferior. I have never once fed into such rubbish. My family and teachers all along the way made me very aware of the fact that I could do anything that anybody else could, as long as I was willing to work hard. I have always thought that I was the equal of anyone. In the "hood" growing up one would never say that he or she let a white boy/girl beat us at anything. At least in me and my sister Jean's cases that extended to academics as well.

Julius Berry. That is the brother who lit the fire of black pride, of dignity of rebellion in me at the age of 15 that has burned with ferocity throughout my life. One night the boys; Geggy, Tony Stevenson, Jake Radford, Smith and I were just hanging out. We were in West End when we just happened to stop by the C.O.R.E. office. This was 1967. So much was going on in the country but we were not politically aware nor were we involved in any ground-roots movement. Julius had been to us a high school basketball legend. We had heard about him for years so we were transfixed hearing him speak. Julius was a tall handsome brother with a ready smile. He wore a fashionable afro. As he began to speak about the wrongs of slavery and segregation we held on to his every word. Then he began to speak about black pride, and nationalism. He spoke about black power and brotherhood. The country was going through a change at this time that we weren't aware of. I had never heard a black man speak like this. He spoke of fighting back. That night Julius changed my thinking forever. There has been, in me, a major conflict since hearing those words. Then, in 1968, the lines were clear cut. It was black against white; or vice versa. It had always been a white against black issue in America. The stereotypical, subservient black man was slowly being transformed into a fist pumping, afro wearing, bearded nationalistic brother who wanted revolution. This type of brother was who I wanted to be. Things were happening in the country which we were just were too young to be aware. We had witnessed the bombing of Dr. Palmer's pharmacy the summer before. Dr. Zirl Palmer was a pharmacist who had opened a first-class drugstore in the Westside Plaza a couple years before. We just were not politically aware. The conflict has been . . .who do I fight? Where are these hooded racists? I had never yet been confronted with the type of racism that I saw on T.V., read about or heard from others. I have wanted to fight this type of racism ever since that night. I have wanted to die fighting against this type of evil since that night. The thing about racism is the subtleness used by the people behind it. It is ever present in the life of black people as a suffocating blanket of oppression. Unless one is caught in the wrong place or under the wrong circumstances, one may never witness racism on the level read or heard about. We grow up, though, being taught to guard against something we may never see. Coming from Georgia I have been taught this my whole life; to guard against something I have never witnessed. I have grown to hate something invisible to *my* eyes.

Our schools were segregated and our communities were segregated but we had teachers who cared for and understood us. There were professionals living in the community to stand as examples for us to follow. We knew that if we did the right thing we could be like Mr. Delaney or Mr. Hughes. They were only two of the great black men who were our teachers at school. We knew we could be somebody because they continuously told us so. There was a constant reminder that we could grow to be

someone if we studied hard and applied ourselves. When there was segregation the black
community was so much more vibrant. We had
a commonality. We relied more on each other
because we had to. This time that I remember
was during the early 1960s. Cassius Clay had
won the heavyweight title over Sonny Liston.
I was in the sixth grade in Mrs. Browns' room.
That's how we would say homeroom. I didn't
know who Derek Stevenson was talking about
the morning he came into class boasting, "Float
like a butterfly, sting like a bee." It must have
been okay because Mrs. Brown only smiled
in a proud kind of way. Later Muhammed Ali
would be the pride of the black community.
We boasted about "Black Power." We shouted it just to hear ourselves say, "Black Power!"
A rage swept the community that has never
left me. To fight the oppressor was going to be
my life's work. I burned with the revolutionary zeal to crush the white man. We thought
revolution was wearing the clothes, giving the
tightfisted salute and talking big. The 'we'
that we speak of, was my little crew. The guys

that I hung out with were poor like me. Some of the fellas had fathers in the home, some didn't. We would hang out and talk "shit," as we called it.

CHAPTER 8

LOOKING BACK ON my life, I can see that race wasn't the cause of our situation. At least not all the time. Race was not the issue that caused the misery in the lives of the black people that I grew up around. The lack of family structure was and is the biggest cause of misery in our people today, as it was for me growing up. I will admit that slavery and the destruction that it wreaked on our families was the beginning of our dilemma, but I won't live with this crutch forever. We as a people can't live with this crutch forever. I can say clear mindedly that dependency on government was an accelerant to this dependency. To me, integration was the most damaging occurrence to the black community in my lifetime. With integration seemed to come welfare and a greater dependence on government. Welfare took fathers out of the home. In my lifetime the housing projects were a stepping stone to middle class living. It became a breeding ground of dependence after integration. I'm at a point in my life now that I can see this dependence as the evil and not racism. I can no longer blame the white power structure for my ills. I must look at myself and the way that I react to the white power structure. Instead of investing in our own communities we thought it better to leave them to live next to someone that we felt was superior. This is the subconscious inferiority that we have as a people. We still won't invest in ourselves and our communities. I will say that a weak family structure was the biggest impediment to my growth as a person. We felt then as we do now that living in a white neighborhood makes us somehow better. This is a sad truth.

Gil Scott-Heron said, 'The Revolution Will Not Be Televised,' and we smoked weed and romanticized the revolution we thought we were fighting.

Time causes us to evolve or devolve. I see men who are today doing the same things that they were doing twenty or thirty years ago. The things I'm talking about are drinking, clubbing, trying to be cool; trying to hold on to their virility even though age can't be escaped. I see the hollow looks, the ashen faces, the emaciated bodies of so many of my lost brothers. A boy needs the guidance of a man to become a man. This is generally a fact of life though there are exceptions. We have so many successful American men of African descent in this country but I feel on the whole we lack numbers. The mainstream media portrays negative images of the American black man throughout the world. So many of our children are influenced by popular music videos portraying our young men as gangster or vulgar or violent. Our young women are portrayed as promiscuous and ignorant. We, as black men in America, have the responsibility to our people to reclaim our rightful place in our family structure. We are the providers, the protectors and the producers for our women and children. It would be so good to make that our mantra for the coming age. As survivors of one of the most dehumanizing of all the social constructs in recorded history, (American and European slavery, (the white man's slave system), we as a people can be considered as the strongest of the strong. We made it through and we must always tell our children the story of this American horror. We don't have to dwell on the story or be stymied by it but we must be aware that the element that harbored such an inhuman system as chattel slavery is still with us today; this year of 2013. The same type of people are among us in this society we live in; we must forever be vigilant, for among the most beautiful flowers there will always be weeds.

CHAPTER 9

I WAS EXHORTING to a couple of my
employees about dependency. Using an analo-
gy of a dog as illustration, I told Carlos and Al,
"You can kick a dog in his ass everyday but as
long as you feed him he will continue to stay
around." I said this to show how too many of
our people have become dependent on government social welfare as a way of life. This dependency has, to me, a direct correlation to the
prison industrial complex that has emerged in

this country. I have talked to young black men who actually feel that it is normal to live a life in and out of the prison system. They have come to expect to be kicked in the ass by life, but at least they are getting fed. They have become dehumanized.

I've been re-reading a book by Kody Scot, a.k.a. Sanyika Shakur the infamous author of Monster Kody's life of a Crip gang member. After watching a few videos of different gang members being interviewed I was struck by the sheer ignorance shown by these young brothers. They are still brothers. They are still brothers albeit ignorant brothers. What reading the book did is make me think of the child soldiers in Africa and how they were kept intoxicated and ignorant. Monster Kody was indoctrinated at an early age and lived a life of murderous brutality and rage without knowing why he was committing self-genocide. These senseless behaviors have been, and is being glamorized on TV and in music videos. We elders of the community have grown either complacent and or afraid to take a stand against what most of us should know as wrong.

Bill Cosby, the actor, comedian, writer and philanthropist was vilified because he spoke the truth about the responsibility of black parents; mothers and fathers to raise our children. My mother taught me; "You can have only one pair of pants but you can wash them and keep them clean." "Taking a bath and being presentable is something we can do." "You don't have to have money to have manners." She said, "Keep your yard clean, pick up the trash, even if you do live in the ghetto." Momma said, "Money doesn't give you values or principles." In the 50s and 60s we were taught so much of this kind of stuff community-wide. "Respect your elders," was drilled into us. With integration came government interference especially in the schools. When corporal punishment was banned in the schools and in the home respect for authority vanished in most children. It was as though white people didn't want black teachers to discipline their children in the school system. We came up hearing, "I brought you into this world and I'll take you out." This was a popular saying in the black community. It was said tongue in cheek with humor but it carried weight. Our parents would beat the "hell" out of us. In a very real way the criminal justice system and now life is beating the "hell" out of our children.

CHAPTER 10

I MUST ADMIT; society taught me to be racist in a way. I can say honestly, that I have never in my life seen a white mob, a white group or even a white person, demean or intimidate a black person simply because they were black. I have not. The race issue has hung around my neck like a heavy weight all my adult life; not from what I have seen or witnessed but more from what I have heard or read. The race issue has been a handicap for me in a very personal way. I have never had a real relationship with a white person. I have had intercourse with several white women but never a real, "get to know you," relationship. The bias that I have been taught has handicapped me in this way. I have never allowed myself to feel anything for a white person or to trust a white person with my feelings. This really is a sad thing to say when I think about it. On reflection I was turned into a predator by the group that I hung with; by the things that I heard, by TV shows that pushed an image of injustice towards blacks, by the history I was taught and by the stories I was told, about white treatment of black people. These things warped my way of looking at the society that I grew up in. I was handicapped by the pictures painted for me by others. My own experience has been different. I just did not see the big boogeyman white boy out there. I have been at war with something that is actually invisible to me. I know that racism exists. I believe the stories of the kkk's brutality and violence. I just have not seen it with my own eyes. I'm always on guard. I try to prepare myself for a war to fight this evil that I've heard so much about.

A steady diet of such books as Ralph Ellison's <u>Invisible Man</u>, Alex Haley's <u>Roots</u>, Frederick Douglass', <u>Mandela</u>, stories of the Montgomery church bombing, Emmit Till and on and on. From my extensive research of history and coming from Atlanta I've been to the Martin Luther King Library and viewed the pictures of lynchings, and even heard stories from relatives in Monroe, Georgia of the Klan riding horses through houses and people disappearing. When one has had these stories and images seared into one's psyche and brain, there forms a hatred not only against the acts but also of the perpetrators of these acts. All of or the great majority of black people that I know have been raised this way. There is in me a fear, but also a hatred for white people. The fear is instilled in you as a young-ster as a protective mechanism. Our parents who came up in the deep south knew of the vicious-ness that could come our way from the white populace if we acted out in aggression or what they would call disrespect for our oppressors. Much has changed during my life but I'm conditioned to always be on guard for an enemy that I've yet to encounter. Growing up though, as I did in the streets, I learned something of guerilla warfare. A warrior must at all times be on guard. One must, at all times watch one's back. At any moment I must be ready for combat. My experience has molded me to be ready to die in the streets of America and I've come to accept this as my fate if need be.

One of the most poignant books that I've read is <u>The Autobiography of Malcolm X</u>. His story is the story that every black man would love to tell for himself. To deal with self is one of, if not the hardest, things I've had to do. Malcolm dealt with himself and evolved into this beautiful king for us as a people. He scared the hell out of much of black population as well as the white. You see, Malcolm had come to terms with himself. I never felt the urge from reading his words to go out and commit a violent act. What I got from reading Malcolm X's story was the realization that to protect oneself is natural. We as black people are justified in fighting to the death an oppressor who will disrespect our women, harm our children or ourselves. To die with honor is better than living in shame. This was Malcolm's message. My sons and daughters will never see me bow and scrape before a white person. My intellect is just as high or higher and my character is just as honorable as any man's; black or white. These are the things that Malcolm taught. This is the legacy that he has left us as black men.

There have been these types of black men since time began but in the history books of America one will come away; after reading, thinking that there were no warriors amongst us. The truth is that the blood of black men has saturated this soil of America in defense of our people. Reading history as told by the conqueror will always slant it to the favor of the victor. These weren't just "crazy niggers" as they would say but noble warriors who stood up to the oppressor to the death. Dying is something that everyone will do but who's to say that living in bondage isn't death? There are those who chose not to live out what the white folks thought was good, "for them" Toussaint L. Overture is only one of many warriors who were victorious over the white man in history. The thousands of great resistance fighters are not listed on monuments in the town square, but they made it possible for us to walk with dignity today.

To think for oneself is the prerequisite to independence. To take responsibility for one's destination is the ultimate goal of every free person. We must reverse the damage done over the centuries to our psyche as people. It is well known that the vanquished usually takes the characteristics of the conqueror; but the case of the American of African descent, we seem to hate ourselves as a group. I look at our women today who seem to think that the standard for beauty is long straight hair like the white women. It's known universally that a woman's crowning glory is her hair. There's no woman more beautiful and regal than a proud black woman who's not afraid to be herself with her own hair. It saddens me to see black women with these long weaves that you know is fake. They've taken on the habits of the white woman in tossing it back out of their face or raking it back with their hand from their eye. The copying of the white woman's features by the black woman shows a subconscious inferiority for their own' hair and features. We as black men must show our honor and respect to our women. They must be held in the highest regard by us first and foremost. We must protect and support our women with all the life in us. Our women deserve this from us for the support and protection they've given us here in America. The black man today is no different in the way we are conducting ourselves. We've allowed our communities to be taken over by foreigners to this country. The Indian and Arab merchants have completely immersed themselves in the taking of capital from the black community. I've observed the disdain in which these foreigners hold the black people who frequent their stores and shops. It's not disdain for us as a people but for how we treat each other; the lack of respect that we hold for each other; and especially how we disrespect our women. We've been portrayed in the media as buffoons, drunkards, shiftless, dishonest and irresponsible and they come to this country's inner cities and that's what they witness for themselves. To stave off the complete demise of our communities we must have enough faith in ourselves to invest in our own communities and in our own people. We _must_ as black men, confront each other in our wrongdoing. Nothing that I've said here is a novel idea but to consistently carry the message of hope for our own people is a must for all who are capable.

CHAPTER 11

OBLIVION BEGAN FOR me as a party. Drinking, fantasizing about being something that I wasn't. I'd always wanted and thought that I would be successful but in life success takes discipline, it takes patience, it takes perseverance and fortitude. My upbringing had ill-equipped me. I didn't know how much family structure meant at the time. The breakdown of the black family here in America is the single most devastating dilemma for us as a people. My parents moving us away from extended family left us adrift in a foreign place. Lexington was home but it wasn't where we were from. There were no aunts and uncles or grandparents when mama and daddy split up. With the hurt and confusion and resentment we were left with; it was like being on a rudderless ship. My siblings and I were adrift in a current of confused emotions. Mama didn't have the strength to navigate these waters with no family to back her. I was to make life very difficult for her and for myself, for my resentment towards her was dealt out with a vengeance. I was traumatized by the split-up of my family and the fact that my father left us in a town where we had no blood family. I call the years that followed oblivion because that's what it was for me. I was lost to the wolf pack of the streets. I was lost as so many black children are today. I was lost to the world of whores, hustlers, dope fiends, killers, molesters and drug dealers. I succumbed to the parenting of the streets. I was lost to the self-induced fantasy of hardness. I thought I was hard inside but the years have made me come to realize that I was hurting inside. All the years of drugs, crime, jail, broken relationships, death and near death and I came to the realization that I was a hurt little boy with no family to turn to. I'm clean now, and have been for years but the therapy continues today. I still try to make sense out of something that makes no sense to this day. I'm able to recognize the obvious state of my black sisters and brothers today because I see myself in them. I see the hurt that is really there and not the hardness.

The saddest and most damaging byproducts of poverty and broken homes in the ghetto is that so many of us give up without ever trying. Poverty beats one's spirit down to the point of impotency. The damage of slavery is still upon us no matter the segment of society that feels that we should just get over it. It's funny the light shined on the plight of the Jews but not black slavery in this country. In the history of man there was never a time when a peoples' humanity has been assaulted in the school books, in the churches and the halls of government as the system of slavery instituted in America. It was taught that Africans were not wholly human.

The institution was inhumane which speaks volumes of those who instituted it.

Even today in the year 2018 we as people have such self-hatred. This is shown especially through our children. The music, the black on black violence. The effect on the black male has been staggering in its effect. It's not a popular subject in American society even among black people but the saying goes; "You reap what you sow." America is reaping as a society what was been sown as a society.

CHAPTER 12

ONE OF THE bright lights of my life has been the narratives of Fredrick Douglass. Across the generations his life has inspired me to not accept my lot because of the hand I was dealt. His lack of a destructive hatred for the white race as a whole opened my eyes to see that we can't judge the actions of all white people the same. Mr. Douglass came through a period of physical slavery at a time when a black man could be legally killed; but stood against this institution.

He has shown that no matter the circumstance of one's life, there is a way if one is willing to make a stand and also make an effort.

As a people Americans of African descent must also accept responsibility as did Mr. Douglass to educate ourselves and our people. We must confront our own wrongs though. I've come to a point in my life that I know the hardest thing to change is me. As a people we must confront the wrong within us. As long as we place blame for our actions on anything but ourselves; as a society we will suffer. Fredrick Douglass though experiencing the horror of slavery firsthand didn't become an outlaw. He didn't become a thug. He accepted responsibility as a man and husband. Even as a slave he pursued honest work. Any young brother that happens to read these words should be inspired by such an example as Fredrick Douglass. We have so many examples who are not and were not O.G.s and pimps and gangsta rappers who really can tell us a thing or two about survival.

CHAPTER 13

"I'M GON DO something to you man,"
Jive told me as I reached to shake his hand.
This was a threat. He'd shaken my partner
Kill's hand. I think he had just gotten out of
the joint. I hadn't seen him since I'd dropped
him outside the Paradise Inn Club. That had
been about a year and a half ago. We were
shooting craps on the side of the building and
he was talking a little too much shit. I was
down on one knee with the craps and Jive got

too close. I reached and snatched his legs out from under him. His boys weren't with him. I had punked his lame ass in front of everybody. I could have dusted him right there in the club. The music was blaring. George Ray, the owner, was bartending. I didn't want any trouble with *him* so I said, "Let's go man," to my partner Kill.

I'd always felt animosity from Jive and his boys from Northeastern Avenue. I was from Hawkins Avenue and always was considered cool. Always.

Jive and his brother Jimmy and their crew may have tried me if they ever caught me wrong but I always watched my back. This all had been back in my earlier years.

As we left the club I saw Jive leave and turn to go up Georgetown Street. He looked as though he may be heading to the Hilltop Kitchen; a club up the street. Douglas Park was directly across from there. I looked at Kill and said, "You drive man." I went around to the trunk, opened it, and pulled out my rifle that I carried. "I'm gone off this nigga man,"

I said as I looked at him. He just looked and said, "Let's go."

I got into the back seat of the car. We pulled out onto Georgetown Street and did a slow pass on up to the Hilltop Kitchen. We passed Jive about a block up the street. He didn't know my car but a lot of other people did. I couldn't shoot out the window of the car. It was night so I told Kill to pull down beside the park on a side street next to the projects called Charlotte Court.

"Be careful man," Kill told me when I eased out into the darkness. Under the cover of darkness I took the rifle and snuck back up towards the front of the park. Staying behind the trees I crept to where I could see the street and waited for Jive to walk up towards the Hilltop Kitchen. There was traffic out on Georgetown Street but it was empty on this side of the park. No one seemed to be around. I got behind a tree and waited in the dark for Jive to walk by on the other side. I tensed when I saw him walking up the other side of the street. My nerves were on fire, my breath was coming faster and I was scared – not of Jive but about what I was getting ready to do. Backing out, to me, would make me appear weak. I had to go through with it.

As he came up on the other side of the street, I raised the rifle and took aim. It was automatic and as I pulled the bolt on the side of the weapon it jammed. Shit! I was shaking but I knew I had to go through with it. Pulling on the bolt I could not get it to push back up to where the bullet would feed into the chamber. Taking the gun down, my chance had slipped by. I eased back to Kill to tell him what was up.

"This shit is stuck, man," I said as I got back into the car.

"Let me see, man," Kill said as I handed the rifle to him. He'd been to 'Nam so he'd know how to work this shit. He tried but he could not unjam the rifle. "I can't get it either Will," he said to me. I'll tell you how we came to be called Will and Kill later.

I don't know if it was an act of divine will or what but that night probably would have changed my whole life had that gun not jammed.

I had to put the rifle back in the trunk and we pulled off. I was actually relieved that it happened that way. I'll never know if I would have had the nerve to actually pull the trigger.

CHAPTER 14

LIFE TAKES SO many turns that one can never make absolutes when speaking. We continue to grow spiritually. I've been baptized but I don't take the bible as literally as so many of my church brethren. In knowing biblical history, I feel somewhat that the translations over the centuries have been altered.

During the late 15th century and early 16th century when the Europeans did their compilations; I feel that the King James version was just that – *a version*. We never take into consideration that one very important word; version. We all have versions of life.

One of the biggest hypocrisies imposed on society is the European picture of Jesus. Children, adults, all of us have grown up with this lie imposed on us. As I've stated earlier history is told through the eyes of the victor.

Jerusalem, geographically, is really in Northern Africa, though it's called the Middle East. Twenty-five hundred years ago, I'm sure, the white population in that area was very small if at all present. The Europeans didn't want it to be well known that civilization went so far back in Africa. One of the truisms from all the religions though is, "You reap what you sow." America, just as the Roman Empire, the Greek Empire and all the great civilizations before them, must face the consequences of its actions.

The thing about race is that it was forced on the Africans, the Indians, and all the non-whites who have faced European domination and the writing of history as they wanted it told. There is beginning to be a backlash all over the world to this dominance and the ways it's been carried out.

On a personal level though I can't condemn all white people. It's just that we as black people, and those that are native American have fared miserably at the hands of the white race. Just as I've stated earlier though forgiveness is probably the most liberating of all things one can do.

There is rage burning in the hearts of black men. It's like a billion small volcanoes within. If these small fires became organized into a mass eruption this country and the world would reap what they've sown. Being able to put this rage into coherent and cognizant thought is the challenge. To somehow bring a positive to the savagery done to the world by the Caucasian peoples is the challenge of 21st century thinkers.

As we age, the thinkers' task is to convey to the masses the commonality of our existence. There are those who've attained power whether by force, ballot box or accident. What's known is that usually power breeds an arrogance which in turn so often breeds corruption.

CHAPTER 15

AS AN AMERICAN of African descent in America one must filter all that's been brought to bear on our psychological makeup and attempt a balanced approach to our everyday life. In the study of nature, one learns that only the strong survive. This is simply a fact. The truth is, it's not color. It's that we all must navigate the labyrinth of our psycho-social walk and exist with a balance that keeps us sane. *If* I'm hated simply because I am black. *If* I'm attacked simply because

I'm black. *If* my social life is altered simply because of my skin color, how do I stay balanced? Just as one reads history. Just as one reads the ancient knowledge of the bible, the world must never forget that which has happened to the American of African descent. Just as the story of the holocaust has been painted, told and retold in American society, so must light be shed on the much worse evil that was and still is a form of American slavery. The world has never before known this kind of evil. It must be written and told just as we read the bible.

This is not to say that the history of America doesn't bother me. I'm sure that I'm pretty much damaged goods because of the bombardment of negative social studies that I've had to endure. Negative but true I must add.

I've gone through my radicalisms. I've studied Islam. I've changed my name. I've called myself a revolutionary in the fight against the white man. I've also gone through the drug addicted lifestyle of disillusionment. I've been to jail. I've been to rehab. I've been so many things. In this book. I hope to be able to find myself.

I'm sure that I typify so many black men in America, absentee fathers, broken homes, abused mothers and children and the repeating thereof. I hope this book will help me and so many of my brothers' tortured souls. On a world scale we are human. We have human faculties and are subject to human responses to learned behavior. I must learn to love myself because I know now that I did the best I could with the tools I had at the time.

"Daddy I forgive you."

"Momma, please forgive me."

"Momma, I forgive you."

I forgive myself.

I must forgive the "white man" if I'm to ever be whole. Today I understand what Martin Luther King was about. He was about the most powerful word in the English language. Love. Jesus said to love one's enemies and to forgive. Get to that. It is so easy to fight, to lash out. We want to hurt someone just as we hurt. To heal though, we must forgive.

These words sound good to me though I know the therapeutic process won't come so easily. I have engrained prejudices and fears. I have learned responses. I suffer as probably every American or for that matter most black or white people do when it comes to race in society. We've been taught to look at color or race. I speak of America because I grew up here and have never lived in another country. This is all I know.

It has been said that if you are not part of the solution, then you are part of the problem. Yes, there are problems in America. Hopefully I can be part of the solution.

CHAPTER 16

MY LIFE OF crime started out as excitement. We would steal a candy bar or ice cream. We thought of this as harmless fun. Never did I dare dream that later in life the same friends I made at the age of six would have done time for murder, grand theft, robbery and running major drugs. A major right of passage in the crime world, and not just in the mafia, is to kill someone. Once you kill there is a respect that comes with it. The understanding is if you do it once you'd do it again. Nobody messes with a killer.

As I look back at life in East End of Lexington, Kentucky, I now realize that a stint in prison was almost expected in some families. This was for the women as well as the men. When I mention East End I mean my life's experience. We were on the poorest streets. It is now known as the "hood."

As long as my father was with us I couldn't do as others did. They weren't disciplined as I was. I was taught religion from Momma and saw Daddy on his knees at night in prayer. My foundation from birth until I was twelve years old was one of structure. In my life this early structure held me together in the long run. As I've gotten older I reflect more and more on what I know now to be childhood training.

We were poor but when one lives in a poor neighborhood the poverty isn't really noticed by the children. We made adventure out of almost any situation. Even in poor neighborhoods there are ethics and morals. There are those who have values and strengths. Religion plays a part in so many of our lives. These are things passed down through the generations.

When I look back on my life, I can remember my Grand-Daddy vaguely. He and Grand-Mama were farmers. I can remember the smell of burning wood, hogs down behind the house, chickens everywhere, cows, and the plow-horse or mule. The smells of country living in those times was wonderful to me. The fresh morning smells of the dew laden woods, the wood burning stoves, and the kerosene lamps all bring a nostalgia to me today of a time gone by. I can remember my grandmother getting water from a spring. I can remember the big black kettle that was used to make soap outside or to boil clothes in washing. The pine woods, and the red dirt of Georgia are embedded in my soul. I come from a father in Alabama and a mother from Georgia. Camphill, Alabama and Lawrenceville, Georgia. I was born at Grady Hospital in downtown Atlanta on January 6, 1952. We left Atlanta for Lexington, Kentucky, in 1958.

Coming up I had my heroes. Jim Brown of the Cleveland Browns, Muhammed Ali, and

Walt (Clyde) Frazier for sports. One of my biggest impressions was that of Fredrick Douglass. Fredrick Douglass stood up against the oppressor at a time when a black man could be killed with impunity. At a time when we as a race were most vulnerable Fredrick Douglas was willing to take a stand and die for it. The fact that Douglas wrote about his life is a testament to so many who died by doing just what he did. The fact is that thousands and thousands of black men and women died fighting against white slavery and oppression.

I had many different mentors. I've been touched by the lives of so many people. I've read thousands of books.

Even though my father drank wine and Momma drank beer I never drank at home in a way to become intoxicated. I was introduced to Wild Irish Rose wine and Thunderbird at the Hilltop Kitchen on Georgetown Street in the West End. I was fourteen years old and hanging out with Gary Anderson, my childhood partner. The Kitchen as we called it was a popular juke joint. This was the "*in*" place for the hip crowd.

I learned to slow dance, fast dance and drink. Ron Young, my West End hero, turned me on to wine. All the guys drank, but Ron was the coolest to me because he could fight. He had a reputation on the West Side like Bangs did on the East side. A fighting rep was what I admired. Dress sharp and drink hard and fight hard. That was the key to stardom in Lexington to me.

The first time I got drunk off of this cheap wine I went home, stumbled all over the house and when I did make it to bed it was spinning in such mad circles that I became violently ill. I vomited until my stomach felt as though it would come out of my mouth. I would never drink again. I knew it that night. The thing with peer pressure is that it will make you do some stupid things. I drank again. In fact, I became notorious for drinking and fighting.

My rebellion as a teen I can see now was an outward expression of an unhappy home. After Daddy left I rebelled against Momma. I had an outward cool and swagger that was only a cover for a very unhappy and insecure kid. I was impotent against a life beyond my control. I was very intelligent which all the more made me realize my economic status. I wanted a secure and happy family so bad that I would fake things at school and to others about the stability of my family life. My solace was that there were so many poor people that I was insulated from the middle class of people. I ran with a gang of boys who were like me in their living circumstances.

CHAPTER 17

I MUST ENTER into my closet to pray.
I must thank God for everything he has done
for me. I must thank God for everything he has
done for my family and this world that we live in.
I pray that my words will help someone in some
way. I pray that my life will not be lived without
someone having benefitted from my existence.

In today's world it seems that if one doesn't
have a lot of money or advanced degrees or titles,
there is no significance to him or her. My life has

been lived in response to what was expected of me so I guess I'm about like anyone else.

I've spent so much of my life and energy focused on the race issue. Being an American of African descent, it is hard not to focus on black and white issues. This has stunted my and so many people's growth. The world's issues are about human issues.

CHAPTER 18

"CHALI, I'LL HELP you if you stand and face your problems. If I help you go to Atlanta you're taking your problems with you. You see, you are the problem," said Mr. Stout. At that moment, without knowing, Mr. Stout was giving me the key to handling the rest of my life. Neither he nor I realized it then but by him not helping me get to Atlanta would make me eventually come to the point that so many had to face. Rock bottom. I had been running for a long time. I just didn't realize that's what I was doing. Louis Stout had always helped me with money and advice. He'd been a friend when I had nowhere else to go.

Mr. Stout was a husband, father, teacher and friend. He had a distinguished career. He became the first American of African descent to head a state athletic association in this country. Louis Stout is known for many professional achievements in Kentucky but I knew him as a mentor and a friend. He cared for me when I didn't care for myself.

What I hadn't seen my father do Mr. Stout was finally trying to make me see. You have to tough it out in life. I'd been told all along the way about seeing things through but I had to come to the point in life where I was at rock bottom. The life I'd lived to this point was one of running from reality. The jolt of self-preservation just hadn't hit me yet. When I say "rock bottom," I mean physically, financially, and spiritually. There was no where to go. I had become a drunk absentee dad. I was an abusive husband. I'd run from any form of responsibility. I was a petty criminal. Through all of this my life was a fantasy to me as long as I had the drugs to escape with. Alcohol was my drug of choice. Cheap and effective. As long as I was high, I didn't have to look at myself. Though I was at rock bottom; it didn't happen overnight. There had been good jobs, clothes, jewelry, parties, women, and cars. Getting to this point in my life had been gradual. What I didn't know at the time though was that getting out would also be gradual.

Looking back now, I know that my choices were the reason for my predicament. At the time though I wanted to blame everything and everybody but myself. One of the hardest lessons for me to learn was to honestly look at myself. The easy way would be to continue on with my fantasy. The fantasy for me was that I was a man. By this I mean responsible, respectful, honest, and hard working. I had not been any of these things on a consistent basis anytime in my adult life. I hadn't gotten there yet but "rock bottom" was coming fast.

When you're in the midst of the storm one only looks at the external situation. Little did I realize at that time that I was the cause of my storm. Everyone could see me but I couldn't see myself. I was running away from all responsibility but lived in a fantasy life of delusion, primarily alcohol but also cocaine and marijuana. I smoked weed all the time and sold it too. At this point in my life I had become a bum. That's the best way to describe myself then.

My street cred' was gone. I didn't command the respect I once had. I didn't have the clothes. My physique, which had always been pumped, was no longer my calling card. I was in a haze. No one could get my attention in a way that would make me recognize myself. I was thirty-four years old, had been married twice, had five children, and had come to this state of being.

CHAPTER 19

"CHALI, WHO DID this to you man?"
"Chali!" Slowly waking and trying to focus and
get my bearings, I squinted up at my brother
Cledi, standing over me. "Where am I at man?"
I asked as I looked up at him.

"You in the hospital man." "Who did this to
you?"

I looked around the hospital room. There
was Smead, my cousin, there with Cledi.

"Who got you Brooklin?" They called me Brooklin from the slang I used when I got out of the Navy.

I didn't know what had happened to me.

"What happened y'all?" "How did I get here?"

"We don't know man," Cledi replied with a frown of concern on his face. "The emergency ambulance brought you here. Ruth called to let us know you were here." My older sister Ruth worked here at the University of Kentucky Medical Center. "They found you in Windburn behind a dumpster." "Where were you at man?"

I couldn't remember what had happened to me. I was hurting. My jaw was fractured. My front tooth was broken. I was pretty messed up and I didn't know what had happened. That is the state I was in. I was walking around in a fog of alcohol, weed and coke.

"Where were you at man?" said Cledi as he continued to look down at me laying there in the hospital bed.

Puzzled; I tried to remember.

"Man, the last thing I remember was I was at this dame Karen's house." This was true. I had fallen asleep at her house. I'd met her one night I was stalking a dude that I wanted to ambush. I'd been following Cincinnati Mike the night she and I met. I'd planned to really hurt Mike. She just happened to be walking in the same direction and we just started talking. No shit. I had a brick that I thought I would bash Mike's head in with. Earlier that night he'd snatched a carton of soda pop from me while I wasn't looking. Long story short, she saw the brick and said, "Boy, I wouldn't want to do nothing to you." "I'ma get this nigga," I told her. One thing led to another and we just hit it off. She was no slouch herself. From under her coat she had pulled a Tech 9. Shit! What had I just walked up on? Anyway, we really hit it off and later that night we'd had sex. At the time she was looking for her boyfriend; I guess to do his ass in. So much for my brick.

"Winburn man, chick named Karen." I was back to the moment. "Okay Brook, we gonna find out what happened," my brother Cledi and cousin Edward said when leaving the hospital room. I'd given Edward the nickname Smead and it stuck.

That assault on me had been the beginning of my turnaround.

Just prior to that my wife at the time had me removed from our house by the police. The officer who came to the house had been a long-time acquaintance. Pete looked sad when he's told me, "Chali you've got to leave man." I was being removed from my home in from of my children. Drunk, I tried to play it off as though I didn't care. The alcohol cushioned the humiliation.

Lying there in that hospital bed I vowed to myself that whoever had done this would pay. Revenge was my impetus to sober up. When I left the University of Kentucky Medical Center, revenge was the fire in my gut. Having no insurance, I left with my fractured jaw untreated.

"Daddy, who beat you up?" My children were wide eyed and fearful looking at my battered face and stiff movements. My wife had allowed me to rehab back at home for a few days. She made it plain that I still had to leave. She could no longer live with the drunken uncertainties that my lifestyle presented.

My brother Cledi and cousin Edward, (Smead) had found out what had happened to me.

I had been at Karen's house. Her boyfriend and baby's father had stopped and found me there passed out on the couch. To this day I don't know what know what transpired or what was said. I'd been blind drunk. He caught me slipping. I was told by a witness that as I walked away from the apartment that evening. Earvin Willard, her boyfriend, had hit me in the back of the head with a bottle. After I fell, I was told he dragged me outside and proceeded to kick me into unconsciousness. I was found by the police lying by the apartment complex. They called the paramedics who had rushed me to U.K. Medical Center. "Chali you know you can whoop that punk assed nigga." My brother Cledi was pissed as he relayed what he had found out about the incident to me. My cousin Smead in his southern drawl laughed and said, "Brooklyn he fucked you up man. "You know you don't want no more of that shit."

More than anything I was bothered that I'd been so drunk, I honestly didn't know what had happened or who had done this to me. I did remember where I'd been though.

"Brooklyn, you'll kick his ass man. Wait 'till you see who this nigga is." Cledi was mad and wanted me to exact my revenge on Earvin Willard. I had to pull myself together and get into shape. I'd been humiliated. To live by street justice, one had to avenge oneself to save face.

More than any other happening in my life, this was the incident that turned me around. It started though with me wanting to save face and get revenge.

After about a week of rehabbing at my wife's house she reminded me that she really did want me gone. Instead of causing a scene and traumatizing my family anymore I packed my few remains and she let me use the van to move.

My world had crashed down on me. I had been many places. I'd been to the military. I'd been a college student. I'd been a promising speaker, writer and performer. I'd also had really good opportunities in my life but alcohol, drugs and the street life, had brought me to rock bottom.

As I drove up Georgetown Street heading to my mother's, where she would let me sleep on the couch, I felt at the end of my rope. This was it. At thirty-four years of age I had sunk to my lowest. There was nowhere for me to turn. Taking that drive in my depressed state I found the only thing I could think of was, "God, I need help."

I had always been an idealist. Though coming from poor circumstances, I never doubted making it in life. It had been instilled in me that I could be whatever I wanted. I never doubted at anytime in my life that I couldn't measure up to anyone. Making bad decisions sidetracked me along the way. When my mother left my father, she also left my rudder. She left the one authority who could steer me. Because I had seen my mother cheat on my father, I blamed her for years. I held a resentment that I didn't understand at the time. The inner turmoil that that I suffered affected every aspect of my life.

School was the first casualty of the break-up of my family. I went from a promising scholar, musician and athlete to a high school dropout at the age of fourteen. My family had split at the start of my most vulnerable years. Puberty. For any youth puberty is a crucial time in life. Lost, would be the most appropriate way to describe me, at that time, and vulnerable.

The breakup wouldn't have been so bad if only my father had stayed involved with me.

I remember the first night we had moved. We'd moved to a one-bedroom duplex on Rand Avenue. Amid the clutter of moving in we were gathered in the one-bedroom. Robert, the man Momma had left Daddy for, was there sitting on the bed. This was the very first night of our arrival. Out of nowhere I remember my father's tall frame just standing there with his arm propped on the door sill. The look on his face wasn't anger. It was more of a smirk. He just stood there blocking the door. My dad was a tall black man. Robert, not as tall as daddy and with a scared look on his face, headed out the back way.

Daddy never said a word. He only stood there a few minutes before turning to leave. I can only imagine what anguish my father had suffered at that moment. That may have broken my father because he later died of cirrhosis of the liver. He was never to be a constant in my life from that moment on. I was to see him sporadically for a year or two afterward but he was never the same to me. My life was to be like that of a pinball for years to follow. I bounced in every direction. There were to be many ups and downs. I didn't know then but depression was setting in. I was a lost 14 year-old boy who had to navigate the seas of manhood alone. My older brother Barry was gone. We had no relatives in Lexington so my uncles weren't there. Robert never was there for us children. I resented him anyway. He never lived with us. I always felt that he was afraid of me. This was my plight.

Looking back, things were not always bad. As children we are amazingly adaptable. There were many boys and girls like me. They say, "Birds of a feather flock together." I'm sure that my circumstances weren't the worst. I've heard stories from acquaintances that let me know my life could have been much worse. Along the way there had been much, much laughter. Along the way there had been joy and thrills and spirited play. There were hugs and kisses. When one learns to take an unselfish look at life it seems to balance out.

I made some choices that definitely could have been better. But if life didn't happen the way it did for me, I wouldn't be the person I am. You see, I've actually learned to look in the mirror at myself in an honest way. I'm not all good; nor am I all bad. I'm human.

We all come into this world the same. A blank slate. We so often become what is fed to us. Out environment shapes us as people. There are those who end up bitter, hurt, disillusioned, retarded mentally and worse. There are those who live a life that can be called normal, but 'life' we all must live. Some adjust to the winds of change. Some not so well. It's been said that life isn't always fair, but it is life.

I happen to be one of the lucky ones in that I came out of life's buffeting as a pretty well- adjusted man. I have my psychological scars but I'm doing well in society. I'm not in jail but I speak in the jail system. I'm an employer. I have issues with my children but so do all parents. Looking back, all the twists and turns, the hurts and pains, the tears and laughter, is what has made me the man I've become. I feel that we all gain wisdom from mistakes. I guess it's the natural way.

I've tried to give a glimpse into the growth of a black man in America. What I've come to know is that my life was and continues to be the same as many, no matter the race. I was affected more by poverty than race. I was hurt more by the relationship of my parents than I was by social issues. My survival had more to do with innate, intelligence, instinct and people along the way who cared enough to be there for me at the right time. There was extended family; people who were not really blood relatives but may have just seen a boy who needed love. Mostly there were teachers who always told me how smart I was. My teachers, along the way encouraged me to strive higher.

I don't know why but even the gangsters I encountered along the way always seemed to respect my intelligence.

My role now is to encourage. I want to always be an example and a witness that one can change their life for the better.

CHAPTER 20

THE SOCIETY IN America in which I learned to survive can be classified as the underworld. This world, this system, this class of people live out of sight on purpose. This is the world of criminal activity. It is so interwoven into regular society as to be invisible to the unsuspecting eye. It's a life and death struggle and it is survival of the fittest. The slickest, the smartest, the strongest and the most ruthless, dwell here. The smartest usually use the strong and ruthless. However, often times the ones who are both smart and ruthless, rule.

I got to know this world while living on what I call the back streets of America. We were the economically poor. So many use this as an excuse. What I've come to realize in my life is that one can make excuses, but more importantly, one can make choices and those choices have consequences. Dealing with the consequences of our choices can sometimes take a lifetime.

There is an old saying, "Live by the sword, die by the sword." More often than not one doesn't want to die by the sword. Finding this truth can be a hard realization.

Rozelle, my cousin, told me that my paternal grandfather's name was Charlie Jones. She said the family came from Camp Hill, Alabama. She said that my grandmother died when my daddy was born. Her mother, Lithy Ann, raised my daddy.

She said Charlie Jones was a blacksmith. This is all I know about my family on my daddy's side. We called Lithy Ann "Aunt Sister." We pronounced Aunt "Ain't." I'm sure we called her that because Daddy would address her as 'Little Sister." She was my favorite aunt. My daddy had other brothers and sisters: Aunt Ruth, Uncle Cliff and Uncle Charles. My daddy's people were tall and dark. My features from my daddy are big lips and a wide nose, with the kinky hair of West African people.

My people were very religious people. I remember the church from a very young age. My spiritual upbringing and discipline carries over to this day, though I no longer adhere to religious doctrine. Spirituality is a way to live whereas religious doctrine is a way to believe.

My story is the story of millions of Americans of African descent in this country called America. The good and evil that came together to produce what is now an empire of imperialism. I have this opinion because what is called freedom is enforced with a gun. My views are enforced by what I research, witness and believe from peoples' testimony abroad. There is great material opportunity in America if one is shrewd, patient, and willing to work hard for it. The freedoms enjoyed in this country are second to none in the world. I say this from research, personal witness and from peoples' testimony from abroad.

I'm moved to share my story because long before me, someone wrote their story and through their experience I came to believe that I could accomplish no matter the circumstances. I've found that there are always life stories that are worse than mine. If one looks to give rather than receive tomorrow just always seems to work out better.

One must be optimistic or the reason for living becomes ever fainter. My optimism burns from someone long before me writing their story down so that I would have hope. My story is to give hope to those who would give up. My story is for someone who doesn't think change is possible. My story is one of survival and I haven't had to kill to make it. My story is one of being an American of African descent and after all my experiences I can give hope. I am thankful for people in my life both black and white. I have friends from other countries who have helped shape my perspective. There is good and bad in the world. What we all can exercise after a point in our lives though is what choices we make. Can we deal with the consequences we make?

This leads me to a time in my life when I had returned from the military and entered the University of Kentucky. I was very much an idealist and thought I could change the world. I could.

It seems like a blur looking back. To sum up the good, the bad, the hurt, the pain, the guilt, and confusion. Yesterday can't be done over. We learn from yesterday to live for today, and to plan for tomorrow. The thing about tomorrow is that nobody knows what it will bring.

I think back on that idealistic boy that I was that day in 1976; standing in the rubble of what had been Stall Pool Court. Though I was the divorced father of two sons, I was still only a boy in my maturity and emotional makeup. I had recently been discharged from the Navy and was now a student at the University of Kentucky.

I was a militant who wanted nothing short of the overthrow of America. I wanted to change the world. I was to learn later in my life one profound but simple fact. To change the world, I only had to change myself. An acquaintance of mine mentioned to me one day, "Chali, I had a paradigm shift." After looking up and grasping the meaning of paradigm; this simple occurrence could have changed my life at a much earlier age. How one sees things can make all the difference in our approach to life.